A Man without a Country

THERE IS NO REASON
GOOD
CAN'T TRIUMPH
OVER EVIL,
IF ONLY ANGELS
WILL
GET ORGANIZED
ALONG THE
LINES
OF THE MAFIA.

A Man without a Country

KURT VONNEGUT

Edited by DANIEL SIMON

SEVEN STORIES PRESS
New York • London • Melbourne • Toronto

A SEVEN STORIES PRESS FIRST EDITION

Portions of the text of *A Man without a Country* appeared
originally in *In These Times* magazine. The author's editor there, Joel
Bleifuss, provided crucial editorial support of this project throughout. The
pieces that appeared in the magazine then became the most visited parts
of the *In These Times* website in the history of that publication.

Others who helped make this book a reality were
Don Farber, Jill Krementz, David Shanks of Viking Penguin,
and, at Seven Stories Press, Dan Simon, Jon Gilbert and Chris Peterson.

SEVEN STORIES PRESS
140 Watts Street
New York, NY 10013
http://www.sevenstories.com

IN CANADA
Publishers Group Canada, 250A Carlton Street, Toronto, Ontario M5A 2L1

IN THE UK
Turnaround Publisher Services Ltd.,
Unit 3, Olympia Trading Estate, Coburg Road, Wood Green, London N22 6TZ

IN AUSTRALIA
Palgrave Macmillan, 627 Chapel Street, South Yarra VIC 3141

Library of Congress Cataloging-in-Publication Data
Vonnegut, Kurt.
A man without a country / Kurt Vonnegut ;
edited by Daniel Simon— 1st ed.
p. cm.
ISBN-13: 978-1-58322-713-8 (hardcover : alk. paper)
ISBN-10: 1-58322-713-X (hardcover : alk. paper)
1. Vonnegut, Kurt.
2. Authors, American—20th century—Biography.
3. United States—Politics and government—2001–
I. Simon, Daniel, 1957– II. Title.
PS3572.O5Z473 2005
813'.54—dc22
2005014967

College professors may order examination copies of
Seven Stories Press titles for a free six-month trial period. To order, visit
www.sevenstories.com/textbook or fax on school letterhead to 212.226.1411.

BOOK DESIGN: POLLEN, NEW YORK
PRINTED IN THE USA
2 4 7 6 8 9 7 5 3

CONTENTS

vii

ILLUSTRATIONS

OH, A LION HUNTER
IN THE JUNGLE DARK,
AND A SLEEPING DRUNKARD
UP IN CENTRAL PARK,
AND A CHINESE DENTIST
AND A BRITISH QUEEN
ALL FIT TOGETHER
IN THE SAME MACHINE.
NICE, NICE,
SUCH VERY DIFFERENT
PEOPLE IN THE SAME
DEVICE!

— BOKONON

I

As a kid I was the youngest member of my family, and the youngest child in any family is always a jokemaker, because a joke is the only way he can enter into an adult conversation. My sister was five years older than I was, my brother was nine years older than I was, and my parents were both talkers. So at the dinner table when I was very young, I was boring to all those other people. They did not want to hear about the dumb childish news of my days. They wanted to talk about really important stuff that happened in high school or maybe in college or at work. So the only way I could get into a conversation was to say something funny. I think I must have done it accidentally at first, just accidentally made a pun that stopped the conversation, something of that sort. And then I found out that a joke was a way to break into an adult conversation.

I grew up at a time when comedy in this country was superb—it was the Great Depression. There were large numbers of absolutely top comedians on radio. And without intending to, I really studied them. I would listen to comedy at least an hour a night all through my youth, and I got very interested in what jokes were and how they worked.

When I'm being funny, I try not to offend. I don't think much of what I've done has been in really ghastly taste. I don't think I have embarrassed many people, or distressed them. The only shocks I use are an occasional obscene word. Some things aren't funny. I can't imagine a humorous book or skit about

Auschwitz, for instance. And it's not possible for me to make a joke about the death of John F. Kennedy or Martin Luther King. Otherwise I can't think of any subject that I would steer away from, that I could do nothing with. Total catastrophes are terribly amusing, as Voltaire demonstrated. You know, the Lisbon earthquake is funny.

I saw the destruction of Dresden. I saw the city before and then came out of an air-raid shelter and saw it afterward, and certainly one response was laughter. God knows, that's the soul seeking some relief.

Any subject is subject to laughter, and I suppose there was laughter of a very ghastly kind by victims in Auschwitz.

Humor is an almost physiological response to fear. Freud said that humor is a response to frustration—one of several. A dog, he said, when he can't get out a gate, will scratch and start digging and making meaningless gestures, perhaps growling or whatever, to deal with frustration or surprise or fear.

And a great deal of laughter is induced by fear. I was working on a funny television series years ago.

We were trying to put a show together that, as a basic principle, mentioned death in every episode and that this ingredient would make any laughter deeper without the audience's realizing how we were inducing belly laughs.

There is a superficial sort of laughter. Bob Hope, for example, was not really a humorist. He was a comedian with very thin stuff, never mentioning anything troubling. I used to laugh my head off at Laurel and Hardy. There is terrible tragedy there somehow. These men are too sweet to survive in this world and are in terrible danger all the time. They could be so easily killed.

Even the simplest jokes are based on tiny twinges of fear, such as the question, "What is the white stuff in bird poop?" The auditor, as though called upon to recite in school, is momentarily afraid of saying something stupid. When the auditor hears the answer, which is, "That's bird poop, too," he or she dispels the automatic fear with laughter. He or she has not been tested after all.

"Why do firemen wear red suspenders?" And "Why did they bury George Washington on the side of a hill?" And on and on.

True enough, there are such things as laughless jokes, what Freud called gallows humor. There are real-life situations so hopeless that no relief is imaginable.

While we were being bombed in Dresden, sitting in a cellar with our arms over our heads in case the ceiling fell, one soldier said as though he were a duchess in a mansion on a cold and rainy night, "I wonder what the poor people are doing tonight." Nobody laughed, but we were still all glad he said it. At least we were still alive! He proved it.

I WANTED ALL
THINGS TO SEEM TO
MAKE SOME SENSE,
SO WE COULD ALL BE
HAPPY, YES, INSTEAD
OF TENSE. AND I
MADE UP LIES, SO
THEY ALL FIT NICE,
AND I MADE THIS
SAD WORLD A
PARADISE.

Do you know what a twerp is? When I was in Shortridge High School in Indianapolis 65 years ago, a twerp was a guy who stuck a set of false teeth up his butt and bit the buttons off the back seats of taxicabs. (And a snarf was a guy who sniffed the seats of girls' bicycles.)

And I consider anybody a twerp who hasn't read the greatest American short story, which is "Occurrence at Owl Creek Bridge," by Ambrose

Bierce. It isn't remotely political. It is a flawless example of American genius, like "Sophisticated Lady" by Duke Ellington or the Franklin stove.

I consider anybody a twerp who hasn't read *Democracy in America* by Alexis de Tocqueville. There can never be a better book than that one on the strengths and vulnerabilities inherent in our form of government.

Want a taste of that great book? He says, and he said it 169 years ago, that in no country other than ours has love of money taken a stronger hold on the affections of men. Okay?

The French-Algerian writer Albert Camus, who won a Nobel Prize for Literature in 1957, wrote, "There is but one truly serious philosophical problem, and that is suicide."

So there's another barrel of laughs from literature. Camus died in an automobile accident. His dates? 1913–1960 A.D.

Do you realize that all great literature—*Moby Dick, Huckleberry Finn, A Farewell to Arms, The Scarlet Letter, The Red Badge of Courage, The Iliad* and

The Odyssey, Crime and Punishment, The Bible, and "The Charge of the Light Brigade"—are all about what a bummer it is to be a human being? (Isn't it such a relief to have somebody say that?)

Evolution can go to hell as far as I am concerned. What a mistake we are. We have mortally wounded this sweet life-supporting planet—the only one in the whole Milky Way—with a century of transportation whoopee. Our government is conducting a war against drugs, is it? Let them go after petroleum. Talk about a destructive high! You put some of this stuff in your car and you can go a hundred miles an hour, run over the neighbor's dog, and tear the atmosphere to smithereens. Hey, as long as we are stuck with being homo sapiens, why mess around? Let's wreck the whole joint. Anybody got an atomic bomb? Who doesn't have an atomic bomb nowadays?

But I have to say this in defense of humankind: In no matter what era in history, including the Garden of Eden, everybody just got here. And, except for the Garden of Eden, there were already all these games going on that could make you act crazy, even if you weren't crazy to begin with. Some of the crazymaking games going on today are love and hate, liberalism and conservatism, automobiles and credit cards, golf, and girls' basketball.

I am one of America's Great Lakes people, her freshwater people, not an oceanic but a continental people. Whenever I swim in an ocean, I feel as though I am swimming in chicken soup.

Like me, many American socialists were freshwater people. Most Americans don't know what the socialists did during the first half of the past century with art, with eloquence, with organizing skills, to elevate the self-respect, the dignity and political acumen of American wage earners, of our working class.

That wage earners, without social position or higher education or wealth, are of inferior intellect is surely belied by the fact that two of the most splendid writers and speakers on the deepest subjects in American history were self-taught workmen. I speak, of course, of Carl Sandburg the poet from Illinois, and Abraham Lincoln of Kentucky, then Indiana, and finally Illinois. Both, may I say, were continental, freshwater people like me. Another freshwater person and splendid speaker was the Socialist Party candidate Eugene Victor Debs, a former locomotive fireman who had been born to a middle class family in Terra Haute, Indiana.

Hooray for our team!

"Socialism" is no more an evil word than "Christianity." Socialism no more prescribed Joseph Stalin and his secret police and shuttered churches than Christianity prescribed the Spanish Inquisition. Christianity and socialism alike, in fact, prescribe a society dedicated to the proposition that all men, women, and children are created equal and shall not starve.

Adolf Hitler, incidentally, was a two-fer. He named his party the National Socialists, the Nazis.

Hitler's swastika wasn't a pagan symbol, as so many people believe. It was a working person's Christian cross, made of axes, of tools.

About Stalin's shuttered churches, and those in China today: Such suppression of religion was supposedly justified by Karl Marx's statement that "religion is the opium of the people." Marx said that back in 1844, when opium and opium derivatives were the only effective painkillers anyone could take. Marx himself had taken them. He was grateful for the temporary relief they had given him. He was simply noticing, and surely not condemning, the fact that religion could also be comforting to those in economic or social distress. It was a casual truism, not a dictum.

When Marx wrote those words, by the way, we hadn't even freed our slaves yet. Who do you imagine was more pleasing in the eyes of a merciful God back then, Karl Marx or the United States of America?

Stalin was happy to take Marx's truism as a decree, and Chinese tyrants as well, since it seemingly empowered them to put preachers out of business who might speak ill of them or their goals.

The statement has also entitled many in this country to say that socialists are antireligion, are anti-God, and therefore absolutely loathsome.

I never met Carl Sandburg or Eugene Victor Debs, and I wish I had. I would have been tongue-tied in the presence of such national treasures.

I did get to know one socialist of their generation — Powers Hapgood of Indianapolis. He was a typical Hoosier idealist. Socialism is idealistic. Hapgood, like Debs, was a middle-class person who thought there could be more economic justice in this country. He wanted a better country, that's all.

After graduating from Harvard, he went to work as a coal miner, urging his working-class brothers to organize in order to get better pay and safer working conditions. He also led protesters at the execution of the anarchists Nicola Sacco and Bartolomeo Vanzetti in Massachusetts in 1927.

Hapgood's family owned a successful cannery in Indianapolis, and when Powers Hapgood inherited it, he turned it over to the employees, who ruined it.

We met in Indianapolis after the end of the Second World War. He had become an official in the CIO. There had been some sort of dust-up on a picket line, and he was testifying about it in court, and the judge stops everything and asks him, "Mr. Hapgood, here you are, you're a graduate of Harvard. Why would anyone with your advantages choose to live as you have?" Hapgood answered the judge: "Why, because of the Sermon on the Mount, sir."

And again: Hooray for our team.

I am from a family of artists. Here I am, making a living in the arts. It has not been a rebellion. It's as though I had taken over the family Esso station.

My ancestors were all in the arts, so I'm simply making my living in the customary family way.

But my father, who was a painter and an architect, was so hurt by the Depression, when he was unable to make a living, that he thought I should have nothing to do with the arts. He warned me away from the arts because he had found them so useless as a way of producing money. He told me I could go to college only if I studied something serious, something practical.

As an undergraduate at Cornell I was a chemistry major because my brother was a big-shot chemist. Critics feel that a person cannot be a serious artist and also have had a technical education, which I had. I know that customarily English departments in universities, without knowing what they're doing, teach dread of the engineering department, the physics department, and the chemistry department. And this fear, I think, is carried over into criticism. Most of our critics are products of English departments and are very suspicious of anyone who takes an interest in technology. So, anyway, I was a chemistry major, but I'm always winding up as a teacher in English departments, so I've brought scientific thinking to literature. There's been very little gratitude for this.

I became a so-called science fiction writer when someone decreed that I was a science fiction writer. I did not want to be classified as one, so I wondered in what way I'd offended that I would not get credit for being a serious writer. I decided that it was because I wrote about technology, and most fine American writers know nothing about technology. I got classified as a science fiction writer simply because I wrote about Schenectady, New York. My first book, *Player Piano*, was about Schenectady. There are huge factories in Schenectady and nothing else. I and my associates were engineers, physicists, chemists, and mathematicians. And when I wrote about the General Electric Company and Schenectady, it seemed a fantasy of the future to critics who had never seen the place.

I think that novels that leave out technology misrepresent life as badly as Victorians misrepresented life by leaving out sex.

*

In 1968, the year I wrote *Slaughterhouse Five,* I finally became grown up enough to write about the bombing of Dresden. It was the largest massacre in European history. I, of course, know about Auschwitz, but a massacre is something that happens suddenly, the killing of a whole lot of people in a very short time. In Dresden, on February 13, 1945, about 135,000 people were killed by British firebombing in one night.

It was pure nonsense, pointless destruction. The whole city was burned down, and it was a British atrocity, not ours. They sent in night bombers, and they came in and set the whole town on fire with a new kind of incendiary bomb. And so everything organic, except my little POW group, was consumed by fire. It was a military experiment to find out if you could burn down a whole city by scattering incendiaries over it.

Of course, as prisoners of war, we dealt hands-on with dead Germans, digging them out of basements because they had suffocated there, and taking them to a huge funeral pyre. And I heard—I didn't see it done—that they gave up this procedure because it was too slow and, of course, the city was starting to smell pretty bad. And they sent in guys with flamethrowers.

Why my fellow prisoners of war and I weren't killed I don't know.

I was a writer in 1968. I was a hack. I'd write anything to make money, you know. And what the hell, I'd seen this thing, I'd been through it, and so I was going to write a hack book about Dresden. You know, the kind that would be made into a movie and where Dean Martin and Frank Sinatra and the others would play us. I tried to write, but I just couldn't get it right. I kept writing crap.

So I went to a friend's house — Bernie O'Hare, who'd been my pal. And we were trying to remember funny stuff about our time as prisoners of war in Dresden, tough talk and all that, stuff that would make a nifty war movie. And his wife, Mary O'Hare, blew her stack. She said, "You were nothing but babies then."

And that is true of soldiers. They are in fact babies. They are not movie stars. They are not Duke Wayne. And realizing that was the key, I was finally free to tell the truth. We were children and the subtitle of *Slaughterhouse Five* became *The Children's Crusade*.

Why had it taken me twenty-three years to write about what I had experienced in Dresden? We all came home with stories, and we all wanted to cash in, one way or another. And what Mary O'Hare was saying, in effect, was, "Why don't you tell the truth for a change?"

Ernest Hemingway wrote a story after the First World War called "A Soldier's Home" about how it was very rude to ask a soldier what he'd seen when he got back home. I think a lot of people, including me, clammed up when a civilian asked about battle, about war. It was fashionable. One of the most impressive ways to tell your war story is to refuse to tell it, you know. Civilians would then have to imagine all kinds of deeds of derring-do.

But I think the Vietnam War freed me and other writers, because it made our leadership and our motives seem so scruffy and essentially stupid. We could finally talk about something bad that we did to the worst people imaginable, the Nazis. And what I saw, what I had to report, made war look so ugly. You know, the truth can be really powerful stuff. You're not expecting it.

Of course, another reason not to talk about war is that it's unspeakable.

3

Here is a lesson in creative writing.

First rule: Do not use semicolons. They are trans-vestite hermaphrodites representing absolutely nothing. All they do is show you've been to college.

And I realize some of you may be having trouble deciding whether I am kidding or not. So from now on I will tell you when I'm kidding.

For instance, join the National Guard or the Marines and teach democracy. I'm kidding.

We are about to be attacked by Al Qaeda. Wave flags if you have them. That always seems to scare them away. I'm kidding.

If you want to really hurt your parents, and you don't have the nerve to be gay, the least you can do is go into the arts. I'm not kidding. The arts are not a way to make a living. They are a very human way of making life more bearable. Practicing an art, no matter how well or badly, is a way to make your soul grow, for heaven's sake. Sing in the shower. Dance to the radio. Tell stories. Write a poem to a friend, even a lousy poem. Do it as well as you possibly can. You will get an enormous reward. You will have created something.

I want to share with you something I've learned. I'll draw it on the blackboard behind me so you can follow more easily [*draws a vertical line on the*

blackboard]. This is the G-I axis: good fortune — ill fortune. Death and terrible poverty, sickness down here — great prosperity, wonderful health up there. Your average state of affairs here in the middle [*points to bottom, top, and middle of line respectively*].

This is the B-E axis. B for beginning, E for entropy. Okay. Not every story has that very simple, very pretty shape that even a computer can understand [*draws horizontal line extending from middle of G-I axis*].

Now let me give you a marketing tip. The people who can afford to buy books and magazines and go to the movies don't like to hear about people who are poor or sick, so start your story up here [*indicates top of the G-I axis*]. You will see this story over and over again. People love it and it is not copyrighted. The story is "Man in Hole," but the story needn't be about a man or a hole. It's: Somebody gets into trouble, gets out of it again [*draws line A*]. It is not accidental that the line ends up higher than where it began. This is encouraging to readers.

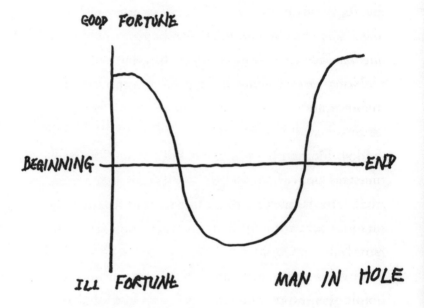

Another is called "Boy Meets Girl," but this needn't be about a boy meeting a girl [*begins drawing line B*]. It's: Somebody, an ordinary person, on a day like any other day, comes across something perfectly wonderful: "Oh boy, this is my lucky day!" . . . [*drawing line downward*]. "Shit!" . . . [*drawing line back up again*]. And gets back up again.

Now, I don't mean to intimidate you, but after being a chemist as an undergraduate at Cornell, after the war I went to the University of Chicago and studied anthropology, and eventually I took a masters degree in that field. Saul Bellow was in that same department, and neither one of us ever made a field trip. Although we certainly imagined some. I started going to the library in search of reports about ethnographers, preachers, and explorers—those imperialists—to find out what sorts of stories they'd collected from primitive people. It was a big mistake for me to take a degree in anthropology anyway, because I can't stand primitive people—they're so stupid. But anyway, I read these stories, one after another,

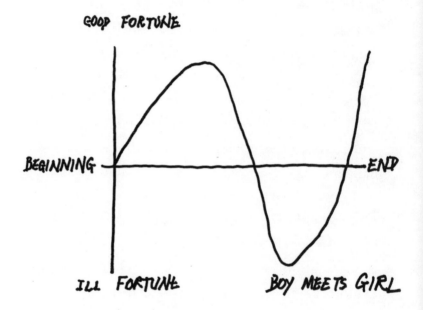

collected from primitive people all over the world, and they were dead level, like the B-E axis here. So all right. Primitive people deserve to lose with their lousy stories. They really are backward. Look at the wonderful rise and fall of our stories.

One of the most popular stories ever told starts down here [*begins line C below B-E axis*]. Who is this person who's despondent? She's a girl of about fifteen or sixteen whose mother has died, so why wouldn't she be low? And her father got married almost immediately to a terrible battle-axe with two mean daughters. You've heard it?

There's to be a party at the palace. She has to help her two stepsisters and her dreadful stepmother get ready to go, but she herself has to stay home. Is she even sadder now? No, she's already a broken-hearted little girl. The death of her mother is enough. Things can't get any worse than that. So okay, they all leave for the party. Her fairy godmother shows up [*draws incremental rise*], gives her pantyhose, mascara, and a means of transportation to get to the party.

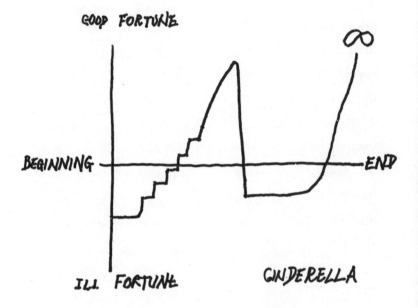

And when she shows up she's the belle of the ball [*draws line upward*]. She is so heavily made up that her relatives don't even recognize her. Then the clock strikes twelve, as promised, and it's all taken away again [*draws line downward*]. It doesn't take long for a clock to strike twelve times, so she drops down. Does she drop down to the same level? Hell, no. No matter what happens after that she'll remember when the prince was in love with her and she was the belle of the ball. So she poops along, at her considerably improved level, no matter what, and the shoe fits, and she becomes off-scale happy [*draws line upward and then infinity symbol*].

Now there's a Franz Kafka story [*begins line D towards bottom of G-I axis*]. A young man is rather unattractive and not very personable. He has disagreeable relatives and has had a lot of jobs with no chance of promotion. He doesn't get paid enough to take his girl dancing or to go to the beer hall to have a beer with a friend. One morning he wakes up, it's time to go to work again, and he has

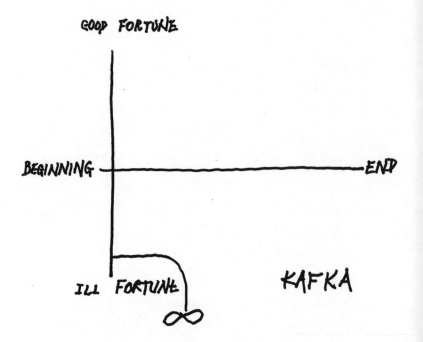

turned into a cockroach [*draws line downward and then infinity symbol*]. It's a pessimistic story.

The question is, does this system I've devised help us in the evaluation of literature? Perhaps a real masterpiece cannot be crucified on a cross of this design. How about *Hamlet*? It's a pretty good piece of work I'd say. Is anybody going to argue that it isn't? I don't have to draw a new line, because Hamlet's situation is the same as Cinderella's, except that the sexes are reversed.

His father has just died. He's despondent. And right away his mother went and married his uncle, who's a bastard. So Hamlet is going along on the same level as Cinderella when his friend Horatio comes up to him and says, "Hamlet, listen there's this thing up in the parapet, I think maybe you'd better talk to it. It's your dad." So Hamlet goes up and talks to this, you know, fairly substantial apparition there. And this thing says, "I'm your father, I was murdered, you gotta avenge me, it was your uncle did it, here's how."

Well, was this good news or bad news? To this day we don't know if that ghost was really Hamlet's father. If you have messed around with Ouija boards, you know there are malicious spirits floating around, liable to tell you anything, and you shouldn't believe them. Madame Blavatsky, who knew more about the spirit world than anybody else, said you are a fool to take any apparition seriously, because they are often malicious and they are frequently the souls of people who were murdered, were suicides, or were terribly cheated in life in one way or another, and they are out for revenge.

So we don't know whether this thing was really Hamlet's father or if it was good news or bad news. And neither does Hamlet. But he says okay, I got a way to check this out. I'll hire actors to act out the way the ghost said my father was murdered by my uncle, and I'll put on this show and see what my uncle makes of it. So he puts on this show. And it's not like Perry Mason. His uncle doesn't go crazy and say, "I-I-You got me, you got me, I did it, I did it." It flops. Neither good news nor bad news. After this flop Hamlet ends up talking with his mother when the drapes move, so he thinks his uncle is back there and he says, "All right, I am so sick of being so damn indecisive," and he sticks his rapier through the drapery. Well, who falls out? This windbag, Polonius. This Rush Limbaugh. And Shakespeare regards him as a fool and quite disposable.

You know, dumb parents think that the advice that Polonius gave to his kids when they were going away was what parents should always tell their kids, and it's the dumbest possible advice, and Shakespeare even thought it was hilarious.

"Neither a borrower nor a lender be." But what else is life but endless lending and borrowing, give and take?

"This above all, to thine own self be true." Be an egomaniac!

Neither good news nor bad news. Hamlet didn't get arrested. He's prince. He can kill anybody he wants. So he goes along, and finally he gets in a

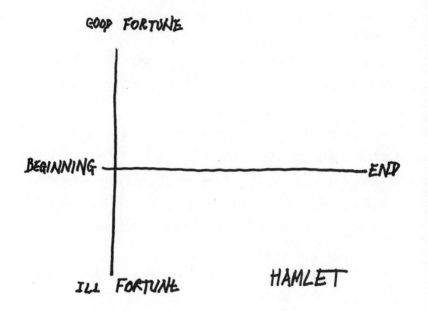

duel, and he's killed. Well, did he go to heaven or did he go to hell? Quite a difference. Cinderella or Kafka's cockroach? I don't think Shakespeare believed in a heaven or hell any more than I do. And so we don't know whether it's good news or bad news.

I have just demonstrated to you that Shakespeare was as poor a storyteller as any Arapaho.

But there's a reason we recognize *Hamlet* as a masterpiece: it's that Shakespeare told us the truth, and people so rarely tell us the truth in this rise and fall here [*indicates blackboard*]. The truth is, we know so little about life, we don't really know what the good news is and what the bad news is.

And if I die—God forbid—I would like to go to heaven to ask somebody in charge up there, "Hey, what was the good news and what was the bad news?"

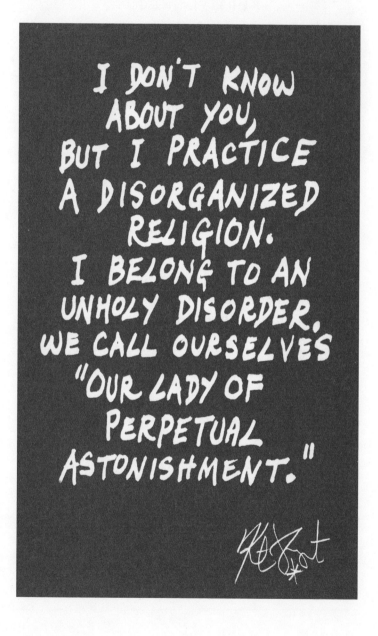

4

I'm going to tell you some news.

No, I am not running for President, although I do know that a sentence, if it is to be complete, must have both a subject and a verb.

Nor will I confess that I sleep with children. I will say this, though: My wife is by far the oldest person I ever slept with.

Here's the news: I am going to sue the Brown & Williamson Tobacco Company, manufacturers of

Pall Mall cigarettes, for a billion bucks! Starting when I was only twelve years old, I have never chain-smoked anything but unfiltered Pall Malls. And for many years now, right on the package, Brown and Williamson have promised to kill me.

But I am now eighty-two. Thanks a lot, you dirty rats. The last thing I ever wanted was to be alive when the three most powerful people on the whole planet would be named Bush, Dick and Colon.

Our government's got a war on drugs. That's certainly a lot better than no drugs at all. That's what was said about prohibition. Do you realize that from 1919 to 1933 it was absolutely against the law to manufacture, transport, or sell alcoholic beverages, and the Indiana newspaper humorist Ken Hubbard said, "Prohibition is better than no liquor at all."

But get this: The two most widely abused and addictive and destructive of all substances are both perfectly legal.

One, of course, is ethyl alcohol. And President George W. Bush, no less, and by his own admission, was smashed, or tiddley-poo, or four sheets to the wind a good deal of the time from when he was sixteen until he was forty. When he was forty-one, he says, Jesus appeared to him and made him knock off the sauce, stop gargling nose paint.

Other drunks have seen pink elephants.

About my own history of foreign substance abuse, I've been a coward about heroin and cocaine, LSD and so on, afraid they might put me over the edge. I did smoke a joint of marijuana one time with Jerry Garcia and the Grateful Dead, just to be sociable. It didn't seem to do anything to me one way or the other, so I never did it again. And by the grace of God, or whatever, I am not an alcoholic, largely a matter of genes. I take a couple of drinks now and then and will do it again tonight. But two is my limit. No problem.

I am, of course, notoriously hooked on cigarettes. I keep hoping the things will kill me. A fire at one end and a fool at the other.

But I'll tell you one thing: I once had a high that not even crack cocaine could match. That was when I got my first driver's license—look out, world, here comes Kurt Vonnegut!

And my car back then, a Studebaker as I recall, was powered, as are almost all means of transportation and other machinery today, and electric power plants and furnaces, by the most abused, addictive, and destructive drugs of all: fossil fuels.

When you got here, even when I got here, the industrialized world was already hopelessly hooked on fossil fuels, and very soon now there won't be any left. Cold turkey.

Can I tell you the truth? I mean this isn't the TV news is it? Here's what I think the truth is: We are all addicts of fossil fuels in a state of denial. And like so many addicts about to face cold turkey, our leaders are now committing violent crimes to get what little is left of what we're hooked on.

What was the beginning of this end? Some might say Adam and Eve and the apple of knowledge, a clear case of entrapment. I say it was Prometheus, a Titan, a son of gods, who in Greek myth stole fire from Zeus and gave it to human beings. The gods were so mad they chained him naked to a rock with his back exposed, and had eagles eat his liver. "Spare the rod and spoil the child."

And it is now plain that the gods were right to do that. Our close cousins the gorillas and orangs and chimps and gibbon apes have gotten along just fine all this time while eating raw vegetable matter, whereas we not only prepare hot meals but have now all but destroyed this once salubrious planet as a life-support system in fewer than two hundred years, mainly by making thermodynamic whoopee with fossil fuels.

The Englishman Michael Faraday built the first electric generator only a hundred and seventy-two years ago.

The German Karl Benz built the first automobile powered by an internal combustion engine only a hundred and nineteen years ago.

The first oil well in the USA, now a dry hole, was drilled in Titusville, Pennsylvania, by Edwin L. Drake only a hundred and forty-five years ago.

The American Wright brothers, of course, built and flew the first airplane only a hundred and one years ago. It was powered by gasoline.

You want to talk about irresistible whoopee?

A booby trap.

Fossil fuels, so easily set alight! Yes, and we are presently touching off nearly the very last whiffs and drops and chunks of them. All lights are about to go out. No more electricity. All forms of transportation are about to stop, and the planet Earth will soon have a crust of skulls and bones and dead machinery.

And nobody can do a thing about it. It's too late in the game.

Don't spoil the party, but here's the truth: We have squandered our planet's resources, including air and water, as though there were no tomorrow, so now there isn't going to be one.

So there goes the Junior Prom, but that's not the half of it.

EVOLUTION
IS SO CREATIVE.
THAT'S HOW
WE GOT
GIRAFFES.

5

Okay, now let's have some fun. Let's
talk about sex. Let's talk about women. Freud said
he didn't know what women wanted. I know what
women want: a whole lot of people to talk to.
What do they want to talk about? They want to
talk about everything.

What do men want? They want a lot of pals, and
they wish people wouldn't get so mad at them.

Why are so many people getting divorced today?

It's because most of us don't have extended families anymore. It used to be that when a man and a woman got married, the bride got a lot more people to talk to about everything. The groom got a lot more pals to tell dumb jokes to.

A few Americans, but very few, still have extended families. The Navahos. The Kennedys.

But most of us, if we get married nowadays, are just one more person for the other person. The groom gets one more pal, but it's a woman. The woman gets one more person to talk to about everything, but it's a man.

When a couple has an argument nowadays, they may think it's about money or power or sex or how to raise the kids or whatever. What they're really saying to each other, though without realizing it, is this: "You are not enough people!"

A husband, a wife and some kids is not a family. It's a terribly vulnerable survival unit.

I met a man in Nigeria one time, an Ibo who had six hundred relatives he knew quite well. His wife had just had a baby, the best possible news in any extended family.

They were going to take it to meet all its relatives, Ibos of all ages and sizes and shapes. It would even meet other babies, cousins not much older than it was. Everybody who was big enough and steady enough was going to get to hold it, cuddle it, gurgle to it, and say how pretty or how handsome it was.

Wouldn't you have loved to be that baby?

I sure wish I could wave a wand, and give every one of you an extended family, make you an Ibo or a Navaho — or a Kennedy.

Now, you take George and Laura Bush, who imagine themselves as a brave, clean-cut little couple. They are surrounded by an enormous extended family, what we should all have — I mean judges, senators, newspaper editors, lawyers, bankers. They are not alone. That they are members of an extended family is one reason they are so comfortable. And I would really, over the long run, hope America would find some way to provide all of our citizens with extended families—a large group of people they could call on for help.

I am a German-American, a pure one dating back to when German-Americans were still endogamous, marrying each other. When I asked the Anglo-American Jane Marie Cox to marry me in 1945, one of her uncles asked her if she really "wanted to get mixed up with all those Germans." Yes, and even today there is a sort of San Andreas fault line running between German-Americans and Anglos, but fainter all the time.

You might think this was because of the First World War, in which the English and the Americans fought Germany, during which the fault opened as wide and deep as a mouth of hell, although no German-American had performed an act of treason. But the crack first appeared around the time of the Civil War, when all my immigrant ancestors got here and settled in Indianapolis. One ancestor actually lost a leg in battle and went back to Germany, but the rest stayed and prospered like crazy.

They arrived at a time when the Anglo ruling class, like our polyglot corporate oligarchs of today, wanted the cheapest and tamest workers they could find anywhere in the whole wide world. The specifications for such persons, then as now, were those listed by Emma Lazarus in 1883: "tired," "poor," "huddled," "wretched," "homeless," and "tempest-tost." And people like that had to be imported back then. Jobs couldn't, as today, be sent to them right where they were so unhappy. Yes, and they were coming here any way they could, by the tens of thousands.

But in the midst of this tidal wave of misery was what would in retrospect seem to the Anglos a Trojan horse, one filled with educated, well-fed, middle-class German businessmen and their families, who had money to invest. One ancestor on my mother's side became a brewer in Indianapolis. But he didn't build a brewery. He bought one! How was that for pioneering? Nor had these people had to play any part in the genocides and ethnic cleansing which had made this for them a virgin continent.

And these guilt-free people, speaking English at work but German at home, built not only successful businesses, most strikingly in Indianapolis and Milwaukee and Chicago and Cincinnati, but their own banks and concert halls and social clubs and gymnasia and restaurants, and mansions and summer cottages, leaving the Anglos to wonder, with good reason, I have to say, "Who the hell's country *is* this anyway?"

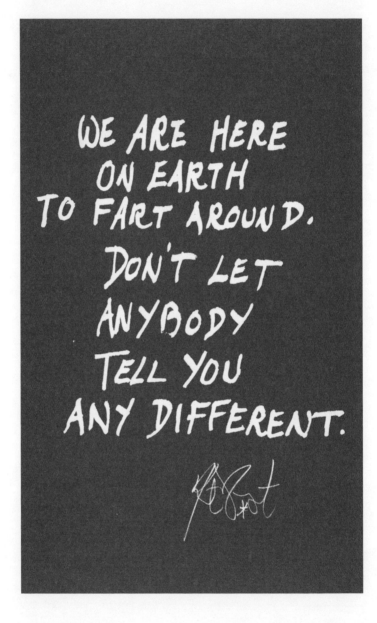

6

I have been called a Luddite.
I welcome it.

Do you know what a Luddite is? A person who
hates newfangled contraptions. Ned Ludd was a
textile worker in England at around the start of
the nineteenth century who busted up a lot of new
contraptions—mechanical looms that were going
to put him out of work, that were going to make it
impossible for him with his particular skills to

feed, clothe, and shelter his family. In 1813 the British government executed by hanging seventeen men for "machine breaking," as it was called, a capital crime.

Today we have contraptions like nuclear submarines armed with Poseidon missiles that have H-bombs in their warheads. And we have contraptions like computers that cheat you out of becoming. Bill Gates says, "Wait till you can see what your computer can become." But it's you who should be doing the becoming, not the damn fool computer. What you can become is the miracle you were born to be through the work that you do.

Progress has beat the heck out of me. It took away from me what a loom must have been to Ned Ludd two hundred years ago. I mean a typewriter. There is no longer such a thing anywhere. *Huckleberry Finn*, incidentally, was the first novel ever to be typewritten.

In the old days, not long ago, I used to type. And, after I had about twenty pages, I would mark them up with a pencil, making corrections. Then I would call Carol Atkins, who was a typist. Can you imagine? She lived out in Woodstock, New York, which you know was where the famous sex and drugs event in the '60s got its name from (it actually took place in the nearby town of Bethel and anybody who says they remember being there wasn't there.) So, I would call up Carol and say, "Hey Carol. How are you doing? How is your back? Got any bluebirds?" We would chit-chat back and forth—I love to talk to people.

She and her husband had been trying to attract bluebirds, and as you know if you have tried to attract bluebirds, you put the bluebird house only three feet off the ground, usually on a fence along a property line. Why there are any bluebirds left I don't know. They didn't have any luck, and neither did I, out at my place in the country. Anyway, we chat away, and finally I say, "Hey, you know I got some pages. Are you still typing?" And she sure is. And I know it will be so neat, it will look like it was done by a computer. And I say, "I hope it doesn't get lost in the mail." And she says,

"Nothing ever gets lost in the mail." And that in fact has been my experience. I never have lost anything. And so, she is a Ned Ludd now. Her typing is worthless.

Anyway, I take my pages and I have this thing made out of steel, it's called a paper clip, and I put my pages together, being careful to number them, too, of course. So I go downstairs, to take off, and I pass my wife, the photo journalist Jill Krementz, who was bloody high tech then, and is even higher tech now. She calls out, "Where are you going?" Her favorite reading when she was a girl was Nancy Drew mysteries, you know, the girl detective. So she can't help but ask, "Where are you going?" And I say, "I am going out to get an envelope." And she says, "Well, you're not a poor man. Why don't you buy a thousand envelopes? They'll deliver them, and you can put them in a closet." And I say, "Hush."

So I go down the steps, and this is on 48th Street in New York City between Second Avenue and Third, and I go out to this newsstand across the street where they sell magazines and lottery tickets and stationery. And I know their stock very well, and so I get an envelope, a manila envelope. It is as though whoever made that envelope knew what size of paper I'm using. I get in line because there are people buying lottery tickets, candy, and that sort of thing, and I chat with them. I say, "Do you know anybody who ever won anything in the lottery?" And, "What happened to your foot?"

Finally I get up to the head of the line. The people who own this store are Hindus. The woman behind the counter has a jewel between her eyes. Now isn't that worth the trip? I ask her, "Have there been any big lottery winners lately?" Then I pay for the envelope. I take my manuscript and I put it inside. The envelope has two little metal prongs for going through a hole in the flap. For those of you who have never seen one, there are two ways of closing a manila envelope. I use both of them. First I lick the mucilage—it's kind of sexy. I put the little thin metal diddle through the hole—I never did know what they call them. Then I glue the flap down.

I go next to the postal convenience center down the block at the corner of 47th Street and Second Avenue. This is very close to the United Nations, so there are all these funny-looking people there from all over the world. I go in there and we are lined up again. I'm secretly in love with the woman behind the counter. She doesn't know it. My wife knows it. I am not about to do anything about it. She is so nice. All I have ever seen of her is from the waist up because she is always behind the counter. But every day she will do something with herself above her waist to cheer us up. Sometimes her hair will be all frizzy. Sometimes she will have ironed it flat. One day she was wearing black lipstick. This is all so exciting and so generous of her, just to cheer us all up, people from all over the world.

So I wait in line, and I say, "Hey what was that language you were talking? Was it Urdu?" I have nice chats. Sometimes not. There is also, "If you don't like it here, why don't you go back to your little tinhorn dictatorship where you came from?" One time I had my pocket picked in there and got to meet a cop and tell him about it. Anyway, finally I get up to the head of the line. I don't reveal to her that I love her. I keep poker-faced. She might as well be looking at a cantaloupe, there is so little information in my face, but my heart is beating. And I give her the envelope, and she weighs it, because I want to put the right number of stamps on it, and have her okay it. If she says that's the right number of stamps and cancels it, that's it. They can't send it back to me. I get the right stamps and I address the envelope to Carol in Woodstock.

Then I go outside and there is a mailbox. And I feed the pages to the giant blue bullfrog. And it says, "Ribbit."

And I go home. And I have had one hell of a good time.

Electronic communities build nothing. You wind up with nothing. We are dancing animals.

How beautiful it is to get up and go out and do something. We are here on Earth to fart around. Don't let anybody tell you any different.

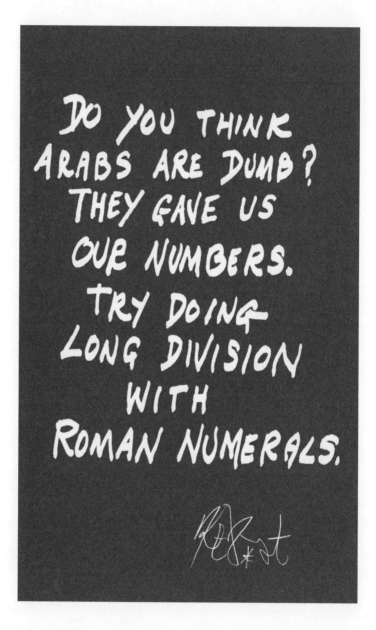

7

I turned eighty-two on November
11, 2004. What's it like to be this old? I can't par-
allel park worth a damn anymore, so please don't
watch while I try to do it. And gravity has
become a lot less friendly and manageable than it
used to be.

When you get to my age, if you get to my age,
and if you have reproduced, you will find yourself asking your own children, who are themselves

middle-aged, "What is life all about?" I have seven kids, three of them orphaned nephews.

I put my big question about life to my son the pediatrician. Dr. Vonnegut said this to his doddering old dad: "Father, we are here to help each other get through this thing, whatever it is."

No matter how corrupt, greedy, and heartless our government, our corporations, our media, and our religious and charitable institutions may become, the music will still be wonderful.

If I should ever die, God forbid, let this be my epitaph:

THE ONLY PROOF HE NEEDED
FOR THE EXISTENCE OF GOD
WAS MUSIC

Now, during our catastrophically idiotic war in Vietnam, the music kept getting better and better and better. We lost that war, by the way. Order couldn't be restored in Indochina until the people kicked us out.

That war only made billionaires out of millionaires. Today's war is making trillionaires out of billionaires. Now I call that progress.

And how come the people in countries we invade can't fight like ladies and gentlemen, in uniform and with tanks and helicopter gunships?

Back to music. It makes practically everybody fonder of life than he or she would be without it. Even military bands, although I am a pacifist, always cheer me up. And I really like Strauss and Mozart and all that, but the priceless gift that African Americans gave the whole world when they were still in slavery was a gift so great that it is now almost the only reason many foreigners still like us at least a little bit. That specific remedy for the worldwide epidemic of depression is a gift called the blues. All pop music today—jazz, swing, be-bop, Elvis Presley, the Beatles, the Stones, rock-and-roll, hip-hop, and on and on — is derived from the blues.

A gift to the world? One of the best rhythm-and-blues combos I ever heard was three guys and a girl from Finland playing in a club in Krakow, Poland.

The wonderful writer Albert Murray, who is a jazz historian and a friend of mine among other things, told me that during the era of slavery in this country — an atrocity from which we can never fully recover — the suicide rate per capita among slave owners was much higher than the suicide rate among slaves.

Murray says he thinks this was because slaves had a way of dealing with depression, which their white owners did not: They could shoo away Old Man Suicide by playing and singing the Blues. He says something else which also sounds right to me. He says the blues can't drive depression clear out of a house, but can drive it into the corners of any room where it's being played. So please remember that.

Foreigners love us for our jazz. And they don't hate us for our purported liberty and justice for all. They hate us now for our arrogance.

＊

When I went to grade school in Indianapolis, the James Whitcomb Riley School #43, we used to draw pictures of houses of tomorrow, boats of tomorrow, airplanes of tomorrow, and there were all these dreams for the future. Of course at that time everything had come to a stop. The factories had stopped, the Great Depression was on, and the magic word was Prosperity. Sometime Prosperity will come. We were preparing for it. We were dreaming of the sorts of houses human beings should inhabit—ideal dwellings, ideal forms of transportation.

What is radically new today is that my daughter, Lily, who has just turned twenty-one, finds herself, as do your children, as does George W. Bush, himself a kid, and Saddam Hussein and on and on, heir to a shockingly recent history of human slavery, to an AIDS epidemic, and to nuclear submarines slumbering on the floors of fjords in Iceland and elsewhere, crews prepared at a moment's notice to turn industrial quantities of men, women, and children into radioactive soot and bone meal by means of rockets and H-bomb warheads. Our children have inherited technologies whose byproducts, whether in war or peace, are rapidly destroying the whole planet as a breathable, drinkable system for supporting life of any kind.

Anyone who has studied science and talks to scientists notices that we are in terrible danger now. Human beings, past and present, have trashed the joint.

The biggest truth to face now—what is probably making me unfunny now for the remainder of my life—is that I don't think people give a damn whether the planet goes on or not. It seems to me as if everyone is living as members of Alcoholics Anonymous do, day by day. And a few more days will be enough. I know of very few people who are dreaming of a world for their grandchildren.

*

Many years ago I was so innocent I still considered it possible that we could become the humane and reasonable America so many members of my generation used to dream of. We dreamed of such an America during the Great Depression, when there were no jobs. And then we fought and often died for that dream during the Second World War, when there was no peace.

But I know now that there is not a chance in hell of America becoming humane and reasonable. Because power corrupts us, and absolute power corrupts us absolutely. Human beings are chimpanzees who get crazy drunk on power. By saying that our leaders are power-drunk chimpanzees, am I in danger of wrecking the morale of our soldiers fighting and dying in the Middle East? Their morale, like so many lifeless bodies, is already shot to pieces. They are being treated, as I never was, like toys a rich kid got for Christmas.

The most intelligent and decent prayers ever uttered by a famous American, addressed To Whom It May Concern, and following an enormous man-made calamity, were those of Abraham Lincoln at Gettysburg, Pennsylvania, back when battlefields were small. They could be seen in their entirety by men on horseback atop a hill. Cause and effect were simple. Cause was gunpowder, a mixture of potassium nitrate, charcoal, and sulfur. Effect was flying metal. Or a bayonet. Or a rifle butt.

Abraham Lincoln said this about the silenced killing grounds at Gettysburg:

> We cannot dedicate — we cannot
> consecrate — we cannot hallow this ground.
> The brave men, living and dead, who
> struggled here have consecrated it far above
> our poor power to add or detract.

Poetry! It was still possible to make horror and grief in wartime seem almost beautiful. Americans could still have illusions of honor and dignity when they thought of war. The illusion of human you-know-what. That is what I call it: "The you-know-what."

And may I note parenthetically that I have already in this section exceeded by a hundred words or more the whole of Lincoln's Gettysburg Address. I am windy.

*

Killing industrial quantities of defenseless human families, whether by old-fashioned apparatus or by newfangled contraptions from universities, in the expectation of gaining military or diplomatic advantage thereby, may not be such a hot idea after all.

Does it work?

Its enthusiasts, its fans, if I may call them that, assume that leaders of political entities we find inconvenient or worse are capable of pity for their own people. If they see or at least hear about fricasseed women and children and old people who looked and talked like themselves, maybe even relatives, they will be incapacitated by weepiness. So goes the theory, as I understand it.

Anyone who believes that might as well go all the way and make Santa Claus and the tooth fairy icons of our foreign policy.

Where are Mark Twain and Abraham Lincoln now when we need them? They were country boys from Middle America, and both of them made the American people laugh at themselves and appreciate really important, really moral jokes. Imagine what they would have to say today.

One of the most humiliated and heartbroken pieces Mark Twain ever wrote was about the slaughter of six hundred Moro men, women, and children by our soldiers during our liberation of the people of the Philippines after the Spanish-American War. Our brave commander was Leonard Wood, who now has a fort named after him. Fort Leonard Wood in Missouri.

What did Abraham Lincoln have to say about America's imperialist wars, the ones that, on one noble pretext or another, aim to increase the natural resources and pools of tame labor available to the richest Americans who have the best political connections?

It is almost always a mistake to mention

Abraham Lincoln. He always steals the show. I am about to quote him again.

More than a decade before his Gettysburg Address, back in 1848, when Lincoln was only a Congressman, he was heartbroken and humiliated by our war on Mexico, which had never attacked us. James Polk was the person Representative Lincoln had in mind when he said what he said. Abraham Lincoln said of Polk, his president, his armed forces' commander-in-chief:

> Trusting to escape scrutiny, by fixing the public gaze upon the exceeding brightness of military glory—that attractive rainbow, that rises in showers of blood—that serpent's eye, that charms to destroy—he plunged into war.

Holy shit! And I thought I was a writer!

Do you know we actually captured Mexico City during the Mexican War? Why isn't that a national holiday? And why isn't the face of James Polk, then our president, up on Mount Rushmore along with Ronald Reagan's? What made Mexico so evil back in the 1840s, well before our Civil War, is that slavery was illegal there. Remember the Alamo? With that war we were making California our own, and a lot of other people and properties, and doing it as though butchering Mexican soldiers who were only defending their homeland against invaders wasn't murder. What other stuff besides California? Well, Texas, Utah, Nevada, Arizona, and parts of New Mexico, Colorado, and Wyoming.

Speaking of plunging into war, do you know why I think George W. Bush is so pissed off at Arabs? They brought us algebra. Also the numbers we use, including a symbol for nothing, which Europeans had never had before. You think Arabs are dumb? Try doing long division with Roman numerals.

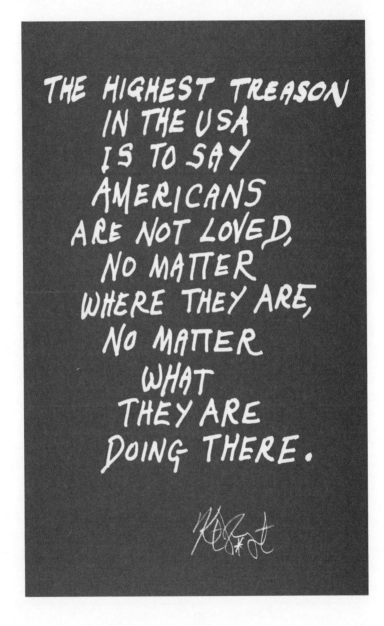

8

Do you know what a humanist is?
My parents and grandparents were humanists,
what used to be called Free Thinkers. So as a
humanist I am honoring my ancestors, which the
Bible says is a good thing to do. We humanists
try to behave as decently, as fairly, and as honor-
ably as we can without any expectation of
rewards or punishments in an afterlife. My
brother and sister didn't think there was one, my

parents and grandparents didn't think there was one. It was enough that they were alive. We humanists serve as best we can the only abstraction with which we have any real familiarity, which is our community.

I am, incidentally, Honorary President of the American Humanist Association, having succeeded the late, great science fiction writer Isaac Asimov in that totally functionless capacity. We had a memorial service for Isaac a few years back, and I spoke and said at one point, "Isaac is up in heaven now." It was the funniest thing I could have said to an audience of humanists. I rolled them in the aisles. It was several minutes before order could be restored. And if I should ever die, God forbid, I hope you will say, "Kurt is up in heaven now." That's my favorite joke.

How do humanists feel about Jesus? I say of Jesus, as all humanists do, "If what he said is good, and so much of it is absolutely beautiful, what does it matter if he was God or not?"

But if Christ hadn't delivered the Sermon on the Mount, with its message of mercy and pity, I wouldn't want to be a human being.

I'd just as soon be a rattlesnake.

*

Human beings have had to guess about almost everything for the past million years or so. The leading characters in our history books have been our most enthralling, and sometimes our most terrifying, guessers.

May I name two of them?

Aristotle and Hitler.

One good guesser and one bad one.

And the masses of humanity through the ages, feeling inadequately educated just like we do now, and rightly so, have had little choice but to believe this guesser or that one.

Russians who didn't think much of the guesses

of Ivan the Terrible, for example, were likely to have their hats nailed to their heads.

We must acknowledge that persuasive guessers, even Ivan the Terrible, now a hero in the Soviet Union, have sometimes given us the courage to endure extraordinary ordeals which we had no way of understanding. Crop failures, plagues, eruptions of volcanoes, babies being born dead — the guessers often gave us the illusion that bad luck and good luck were understandable and could somehow be dealt with intelligently and effectively. Without that illusion, we all might have surrendered long ago.

But the guessers, in fact, knew no more than the common people and sometimes less, even when, or especially when, they gave us the illusion that we were in control of our destinies.

Persuasive guessing has been at the core of leadership for so long, for all of human experience so far, that it is wholly unsurprising that most of the leaders of this planet, in spite of all the information that is suddenly ours, want the guessing to go on. It is now their turn to guess and guess and be listened to. Some of the loudest, most proudly ignorant guessing in the world is going on in Washington today. Our leaders are sick of all the solid information that has been dumped on humanity by research and scholarship and investigative reporting. They think that the whole country is sick of it, and they could be right. It isn't the gold standard that they want to put us back on. They want something even more basic. They want to put us back on the snake-oil standard.

Loaded pistols are good for everyone except inmates in prisons or lunatic asylums.

That's correct.

Millions spent on public health are inflationary.

That's correct.

Billions spent on weapons will bring inflation down.

That's correct.

Dictatorships to the right are much closer to American ideals than dictatorships to the left.

That's correct.

The more hydrogen bomb warheads we have,

all set to go off at a moment's notice, the safer humanity is and the better off the world will be that our grandchildren will inherit.

That's correct.

Industrial wastes, and especially those that are radioactive, hardly ever hurt anybody, so everybody should shut up about them.

That's correct.

Industries should be allowed to do whatever they want to do: Bribe, wreck the environment just a little, fix prices, screw dumb customers, put a stop to competition, and raid the Treasury when they go broke.

That's correct.

That's free enterprise.

And that's correct.

The poor have done something very wrong or they wouldn't be poor, so their children should pay the consequences.

That's correct.

The United States of America cannot be expected to look after its own people.

That's correct.

The free market will do that.

That's correct.

The free market is an automatic system of justice.

That's correct.

I'm kidding.

And if you actually are an educated, thinking person, you will not be welcome in Washington, D.C. I know a couple of bright seventh graders who would not be welcome in Washington, D.C. Do you remember those doctors a few months back who got together and announced that it was a simple, clear medical fact that we could not survive even a moderate attack by hydrogen bombs? They were not welcome in Washington, D.C.

Even if we fired the first salvo of hydrogen weapons and the enemy never fired back, the poisons released would probably kill the whole planet by and by.

What is the response in Washington? They guess otherwise. What good is an education? The boisterous guessers are still in charge—the haters of information. And the guessers are almost all highly educated people. Think of that. They have had to throw away their educations, even Harvard or Yale educations.

If they didn't do that, there is no way their uninhibited guessing could go on and on and on. Please, don't you do that. But if you make use of the vast fund of knowledge now available to educated persons, you are going to be lonesome as hell. The guessers outnumber you—and now I have to guess—about ten to one.

In case you haven't noticed, as the result of a shamelessly rigged election in Florida, in which thousands of African Americans were arbitrarily disenfranchised, we now present ourselves to the rest of the world as proud, grinning, jut-jawed, pitiless war-lovers with appallingly powerful weaponry—who stand unopposed.

In case you haven't noticed, we are now as feared and hated all over the world as the Nazis once were.

And with good reason.

In case you haven't noticed, our unelected leaders have dehumanized millions and millions of human beings simply because of their religion and race. We wound 'em and kill 'em and torture 'em and imprison 'em all we want.

Piece of cake.

In case you haven't noticed, we also dehumanized our own soldiers, not because of their religion or race, but because of their low social class.

Send 'em anywhere. Make 'em do anything.

Piece of cake.

The O'Reilly Factor.

So I am a man without a country, except for the librarians and a Chicago paper called *In These Times*.

Before we attacked Iraq, the majestic *New York Times* guaranteed that there were weapons of mass destruction there.

Albert Einstein and Mark Twain gave up on the human race at the end of their lives, even though Twain hadn't even seen the First World War. War is now a form of TV entertainment, and what made the First World War so particularly entertaining were two American inventions, barbed wire and the machine gun.

Shrapnel was invented by an Englishman of the same name. Don't you wish you could have something named after you?

Like my distinct betters Einstein and Twain, I now give up on people, too. I am a veteran of the Second World War and I have to say this is not the first time I have surrendered to a pitiless war machine.

My last words? "Life is no way to treat an animal, not even a mouse."

Napalm came from Harvard. *Veritas!*

Our president is a Christian? So was Adolf Hitler.

What can be said to our young people, now that psychopathic personalities, which is to say persons without consciences, without senses of pity or shame, have taken all the money in the treasuries of our government and corporations, and made it all their own?

*

And the most I can give you to cling to is a poor thing, actually. Not much better than nothing, and maybe it's a little worse than nothing. It is the idea of a truly modern hero. It is the bare bones of the life of Ignaz Semmelweis, my hero.

Ignaz Semmelweis was born in Budapest in 1818. His life overlapped with that of my grandfather and with that of your grandfathers, and it may seem a long time ago, but actually he lived only yesterday.

He became an obstetrician, which should make him modern hero enough. He devoted his life to the health of babies and mothers. We could use more heroes like that. There's damn little caring for mothers, babies, old people, or anybody physically or economically weak these days as we become ever more industrialized and militarized with the guessers in charge.

I have said to you how new all this information is. It is so new that the idea that many diseases are caused by germs is only about 140 years old. The house I own in Sagaponack, Long Island, is nearly twice that old. I don't know how they lived long enough to finish it. I mean, the germ theory is really recent. When my father was a little boy, Louis Pasteur was still alive and still plenty controversial. There were still plenty of high-powered guessers who were furious at people who would listen to him instead of to them.

Yes, and Ignaz Semmelweis also believed that germs could cause diseases. He was horrified when he went to work for a maternity hospital in Vienna, Austria, to find out that one mother in ten was dying of childbed fever.

These were poor people—rich people still had their babies at home. Semmelweis observed hospital routines, and began to suspect that doctors were bringing the infection to the patients. He noticed that the doctors often went directly from dissecting corpses in the morgue to examining mothers in the maternity ward. He suggested as an experiment that the doctors wash their hands before touching the mothers.

What could be more insulting? How dare he make such a suggestion to his social superiors? He was a nobody, he realized. He was from out of town, with no friends and protectors among the Austrian nobility. But all that dying went on and on, and Semmelweis, having far less sense about how to get along with others in this world than you and I would have, kept on asking his colleagues to wash their hands.

They at last agreed to do this in a spirit of lampoonery, of satire, of scorn. How they must have lathered and lathered and scrubbed and scrubbed and cleaned under their fingernails.

The dying stopped—imagine that! The dying stopped. He saved all those lives.

Subsequently, it might be said that he has saved millions of lives—including, quite possibly, yours and mine. What thanks did Semmelweis get from the leaders of his profession in Viennese society, guessers all? He was forced out of the hospital and out of Austria itself, whose people he had served so well. He finished his career in a provincial hospital in Hungary. There he gave up on humanity—which is us, and our information-age knowledge—and on himself.

One day, in the dissecting room, he took the blade of a scalpel with which he had been cutting up a corpse, and he stuck it on purpose into the palm of his hand. He died, as he knew he would, of blood poisoning soon afterward.

The guessers had had all the power. They had won again. Germs indeed. The guessers revealed something else about themselves, too, which we should duly note today. They aren't really interested in saving lives. What matters to them is being listened to—as, however ignorantly, their guessing goes on and on and on. If there's anything they hate, it's a wise human.

So be one anyway. Save our lives and your lives, too. Be honorable.

WE DO, DOODLEY DO,
DOODLEY DO, DOODLEY DO,
WHAT WE MUST,
MUDDILY MUST,
MUDDILY MUST,
MUDDILY MUST,

UNTIL WE BUST,
BODILY BUST,
BODILY BUST,
BODILY BUST.

— BOKONON

9

"Do unto others what you would have them do unto you." A lot of people think Jesus said that, because it is so much the sort of thing Jesus liked to say. But it was actually said by Confucius, a Chinese philosopher, five hundred years before there was that greatest and most humane of human beings, named Jesus Christ.

The Chinese also gave us, via Marco Polo, pasta and the formula for gunpowder. The

Chinese were so dumb they only used gunpowder for fireworks. And everybody was so dumb back then that nobody in either hemisphere even knew that there was another one.

We've sure come a long way since then. Sometimes I wish we hadn't. I hate H-bombs and the Jerry Springer Show.

But back to people like Confucius and Jesus and my son the doctor, Mark, each of whom have said in their own way how we could behave more humanely and maybe make the world a less painful place. One of my favorite humans is Eugene Debs, from Terre Haute in my native state of Indiana.

Get a load of this. Eugene Debs, who died back in 1926, when I was not yet four, ran five times as the Socialist Party candidate for president, winning 900,000 votes, almost 6 percent of the popular vote, in 1912, if you can imagine such a ballot. He had this to say while campaigning:

As long as there is a lower class, I am in it.
As long as there is a criminal element, I'm of it.

As long as there is a soul in prison, I am not free.

Doesn't anything socialistic make you want to throw up? Like great public schools, or health insurance for all?

When you get out of bed each morning, with the roosters crowing, wouldn't you like to say. "As long as there is a lower class, I am in it. As long as there is a criminal element, I am of it. As long as there is a soul in prison, I am not free."

How about Jesus' Sermon on the Mount, the Beatitudes?

Blessed are the meek, for they shall inherit the Earth.
Blessed are the merciful, for they shall obtain mercy.
Blessed are the peacemakers, for they shall be
    called the children of God.

And so on.

Not exactly planks in a Republican platform. Not exactly George W. Bush, Dick Cheney, or Donald Rumsfeld stuff.

For some reason, the most vocal Christians among us never mention the Beatitudes. But, often with tears in their eyes, they demand that the Ten Commandments be posted in public buildings. And of course that's Moses, not Jesus. I haven't heard one of them demand that the Sermon on the Mount, the Beatitudes, be posted anywhere.

"Blessed are the merciful" in a courtroom? "Blessed are the peacemakers" in the Pentagon? Give me a break!

It so happens that idealism enough for anyone is not made of perfumed pink clouds. It is the law! It is the U.S. Constitution.

But I myself feel that our country, for whose Constitution I fought in a just war, might as well have been invaded by Martians and body snatchers. Sometimes I wish it had been. What has happened instead is that it was taken over by means of the sleaziest, low-comedy, Keystone Cops-style coup d'état imaginable.

I was once asked if I had any ideas for a really scary reality TV show. I have one reality show that would really make your hair stand on end: "C-Students from Yale."

George W. Bush has gathered around him upper-crust C-students who know no history or geography, plus not-so-closeted white supremacists, aka Christians, and plus, most frighteningly, psychopathic personalities, or PPs, the medical term for smart, personable people who have no consciences.

To say somebody is a PP is to make a perfectly respectable diagnosis, like saying he or she has appendicitis or athlete's foot. The classic medical text on PPs is *The Mask of Sanity* by Dr. Hervey Cleckley, a clinical professor of psychiatry at the Medical College of Georgia, and published in 1941. Read it!

Some people are born deaf, some are born blind or whatever, and this book is about congenitally defective human beings of a sort that is making this whole country and many other parts of the planet go completely haywire nowadays. These were people born without consciences, and suddenly they are taking charge of everything.

PPs are presentable, they know full well the suffering their actions may cause others, but they do not care. They cannot care because they are nuts. They have a screw loose!

And what syndrome better describes so many executives at Enron and WorldCom and on and on, who have enriched themselves while ruining their employees and investors and country and who still feel as pure as the driven snow, no matter what anybody may say to or about them? And they are waging a war that is making billionaires out of millionaires, and trillionaires out of billionaires, and they own television, and they bankroll George Bush, and not because he's against gay marriage.

So many of these heartless PPs now hold big jobs in our federal government, as though they were leaders instead of sick. They have taken charge. They have taken charge of communications and the schools, so we might as well be Poland under occupation.

They might have felt that taking our country into an endless war was simply something decisive to do. What has allowed so many PPs to rise so high in corporations, and now in government, is that they are so decisive. They are going to do something every fuckin' day and they are not afraid. Unlike normal people, they are never filled with doubts, for the simple reason that they don't give a fuck what happens next. Simply can't. Do this! Do that! Mobilize the reserves! Privatize the public schools! Attack Iraq! Cut health care! Tap everybody's telephone! Cut taxes on the rich! Build a trillion-dollar missile shield! Fuck habeas corpus and the Sierra Club and *In These Times*, and kiss my ass!

There is a tragic flaw in our precious Constitution, and I don't know what can be done to fix it. This is it:

Only nut cases want to be president. This was true even in high school. Only clearly disturbed people ran for class president.

The title of Michael Moore's *Fahrenheit* 9/11 is a parody of the title of Ray Bradbury's great science-fiction novel *Fahrenheit 451*. Four hundred and fifty-one degrees Fahrenheit is the combustion point, incidentally, of paper, of which books are composed. The hero of Bradbury's novel is a municipal worker whose job is burning books.

While on the subject of burning books, I want to congratulate librarians, not famous for their physical strength, their powerful political connections or great wealth, who, all over this country, have staunchly resisted anti-democratic bullies who have tried to remove certain books from their shelves, and destroyed records rather than have to reveal to thought police the names of persons who have checked out those titles.

So the America I loved still exists, if not in the White House, the Supreme Court, the Senate, the House of Representatives, or the media. The America I loved still exists at the front desks of our public libraries.

And still on the subject of books: Our daily news sources, newspapers and TV, are now so craven, so unvigilant on behalf of the American people, so uninformative, that only in books do we learn what's really going on.

I will cite an example: *House of Bush, House of Saud* by Craig Unger, published in early 2004, that humiliating, shameful, blood-soaked year.

THAT'S THE END OF
GOOD NEWS ABOUT
ANYTHING. OUR
PLANET'S IMMUNE
SYSTEM IS TRYING
TO GET RID OF
PEOPLE. THIS IS
SURE THE WAY TO
DO THAT.

KV

6 AM   11/3/04

10

A sappy woman from Ypsilanti sent me
a letter a few years back. She knew I was sappy,
too, which is to say a lifelong northern Democrat
in the Franklin Delano Roosevelt tradition,
a friend of the working stiffs. She was about
to have a baby—not mine—and she wanted
to know if it was a bad thing to bring such a
sweet and innocent creature into a world as bad
as this one.

She wrote, "I'd love to know your thoughts for a woman of 43 who is finally going to have a child but is wary of bringing a new life into such a frightening world."

Don't do it! I wanted to tell her. It could be another George W. Bush or Lucrezia Borgia. The kid would be lucky to be born into a society where even the poor people are overweight but unlucky to be in one without a national health plan or decent public education for most, where lethal injection and warfare are forms of entertainment, and where it costs an arm and a leg to go to college. This would not be the case if the kid were a Canuck or Swede or Limey or Frog or Kraut. So either go on practicing safe sex or emigrate.

But I replied that what made being alive almost worthwhile for me, besides music, was all the saints I met, who could be anywhere. By saints I meant people who behaved decently in a strikingly indecent society.

Joe, a young man from Pittsburg, came up to me with one request: "Please tell me it will all be okay."

"Welcome to Earth, young man," I said. "It's hot in the summer and cold in the winter. It's round and wet and crowded. At the outside, Joe, you've got about a hundred years here. There's only one rule that I know of: Goddamn it, Joe, you've got to be kind!"

A young man in Seattle recently wrote me:

> The other day I was asked to do the now common act of taking off my shoes at the airport security screening. As I deposited my shoes in the tray, a sense of utter absurdity washed over me. I have to take my shoes off and have them scanned by an X-ray machine because some guy tried to blow up an airliner with his sneakers. And I thought, I feel like I'm in a world not

even Kurt Vonnegut could have imagined. So now that I find I can ask you such questions, tell me, could you have imagined it? (We're in real trouble if someone figures out how to make explosive pants.)

I wrote back:

The shoe thing at the airports and Code Orange and so on are world-class practical jokes, all right. But my all-time favorite is one the holy, anti-war clown Abbie Hoffman (1936–1989) pulled off during the Vietnam War. He announced that the new high was banana peels taken rectally. So then FBI scientists stuffed banana peels up their asses to find out if this was true or not. Or so we hoped.

People are so afraid. Take the man, with no address, who wrote:

If you knew that a man posed a danger to you—maybe he had a gun in his pocket, and you felt that he would not hesitate one moment to use it on you—what would you do? We know Iraq poses a threat to us, to the rest of the world. Why do we sit here and pretend we are protected? That is exactly what happened with al-Qaeda and 9/11. With Iraq, though, the threat is on a much larger scale. Should we sit back, be little children that sit in fear and just wait?

I wrote back:

Please, for the sake of us all, get a shotgun, preferably a 12-gauge double-barrel, and right there in your own neighborhood blow off the heads of people, cops excepted, who may be armed.

A man from Little Deer Isle, Maine wrote me and asked:

What genuinely motivates al-Qaeda to kill and self-destruct? The president says, "They hate our freedoms"—our freedom of religion, our freedom of speech, our freedom to vote and assemble and disagree with each other, which surely is not what has been learned from the captives being held in Guantanamo, or what he is told in his briefings. Why do the communications industry and our elected politicians allow Bush to get away with such nonsense? And how can there ever be peace, and even trust in our leaders, if the American people aren't told the truth?

Well, one wishes that those who took over our federal government, and hence the world, by means of a Mickey Mouse coup d'état, who disconnected all the burglar alarms prescribed by the Constitution, which is to say the House and Senate, and the Supreme Court, and We, the

People, were truly Christian. But as William Shakespeare told us long ago, "The devil can cite Scripture for his purpose."

Or as a man from San Francisco put it in a letter to me:

> How can the American public be so stupid? People still believe that Bush was elected, that he cares about us and has some idea of what he is doing. How can we "save" people by killing them and destroying their country? How can we strike first on the belief that we will soon be attacked? No sense, no reason, no moral grounds have gotten through to him. He is nothing but a moron puppet leading us all over the precipice. Why can't people see that the military dictator in the White House has no clothes?

I told him that if he doubted that we are demons in Hell, he should read *The Mysterious Stranger*, which Mark Twain wrote in 1898, long before the First World War (1914–1918). In the title story he proves to his own grim satisfaction, and to mine as well, that Satan and not God created the planet earth and "the damned human race." If you doubt that, read your morning paper. Never mind what paper. Never mind what date.

WHAT IS IT,
WHAT CAN IT
POSSIBLY BE
ABOUT
BLOW JOBS
AND GOLF?

— MARTIAN VISITOR.

11

Now then, I have some good news for you and some bad news. The bad news is that the Martians have landed in New York City and are staying at the Waldorf Astoria. The good news is that they only eat homeless men, women, and children of all colors, and they pee gasoline.

Put that pee in a Ferrari, and you can go a hundred miles an hour. Put some in an airplane, and you can go as fast as a bullet and drop all kinds of crap on Arabs. Put some in a school bus, and it'll get the kids to and from school. Put some in a fire engine, and it will get firemen to the fire so they can put the fire out. Put some in a Honda, and it'll get you to work and then back home again.

And wait until you hear what the Martians poop. It's uranium. Just one of them can light and heat every home and school and church and business in Tacoma.

But seriously, if you keep up with current events in the supermarket tabloids, you know that a team of Martian anthropologists has been studying our culture for the past ten years, since our culture is the only one worth a nickel on the whole planet. You can sure forget Brazil and Argentina.

Anyway, they went home last week, because they knew how terrible global warming was about to become. Their space vehicle, incidentally, wasn't a flying saucer. It was more like a flying soup tureen. And they're little all right, only six inches high. But they are not green. They're mauve.

And their little mauve leader, by way of farewell, said in that teeny-weeny, tanny-wanny, toney little voice of hers that there were two things about American culture no Martian would ever understand.

"What is it," she squeaked, "what can it possibly be about blowjobs and golf?"

That is stuff from a novel I've been working on for the past five years, about Gil Berman, thirty-six years my junior, a standup comedian at the end of the world. It is about making jokes while we are killing all the fish in the ocean, and touching off the last chunks or drops or whiffs of fossil fuel. But it will not let itself be finished.

Its working title—or actually, its nonworking title—is *If God Were Alive Today*. And hey, listen, it is time we thanked God that we are in a country where even the poor people are overweight. But the Bush diet could change that.

And about the novel I can never finish, *If God Were Alive Today*, the hero, the stand-up comedian on Doomsday, not only does he denounce our addiction to fossil fuels and the pushers in the White House, because of overpopulation he is also against sexual intercourse. Gil Berman tells his audiences:

> I have become a flaming neuter. I am as celibate as at least fifty percent of the heterosexual Roman Catholic clergy. And celibacy is no root canal. It's so cheap and convenient. Talk about safe sex! You don't have to do anything afterwards, because there is no afterward.
>
> And when my tantrum, which is what I call my TV set, flashes boobs and smiles in my face, and says everybody but me is going to get laid tonight, and this is a national emergency, so I've got to rush out and buy a car or pills, or a folding gymnasium that I can hide under my bed, I laugh like a hyena. I know and you know that millions and millions of good Americans, present company not excepted, are not going to get laid tonight.
>
> And we flaming neuters vote! I look forward to a day when the President of the United States, no less, who probably isn't going to get laid tonight

either, decrees a National Neuter Pride Day. Out of our closets we'll come by the millions. Shoulders squared, chins held high, we'll go marching up Main Streets all over this boob-crazed democracy of ours, laughing like hyenas.

What about God? If He were alive today? Gil Berman says, "God would have to be an atheist, because the excrement has hit the air-conditioning big time, big time."

*

I think one of the biggest mistakes we're making, second only to being people, has to do with what time really is. We have all these instruments for slicing it up like a salami, clocks and calendars, and we name the slices as though we own them, and they can never change—"11:00 AM, November 11, 1918," for example—when in fact they are as likely to break into pieces or go scampering off as dollops of mercury.

Might not it be possible, then, that the Second World War was a cause of the first one? Otherwise, the first one remains inexplicable nonsense of the most gruesome kind. Or try this: Is it possible that seemingly incredible geniuses like Bach and Shakespeare and Einstein were not in fact super-human, but simply plagiarists, copying great stuff from the future?

On Tuesday, January 20, 2004, I sent Joel Bleifuss, my editor at *In These Times*, this fax:

ON ORANGE ALERT HERE.

ECONOMIC TERRORIST ATTACK

EXPECTED AT 8 PM EST. KV

Worried, he called, asking what was up. I said I would tell him when I had more complete information on the bombs George Bush was set to deliver in his State of the Union address.

That night I got a call from my friend, the out-of-print-science-fiction writer Kilgore Trout. He asked me, "Did you watch the State of the Union address?"

"Yes, and it certainly helped to remember what the great British socialist playwright George Bernard Shaw said about this planet."

"Which was?"

"He said, 'I don't know if there are men on the moon, but if there are, they must be using the earth as their lunatic asylum.' And he wasn't talking about the germs or the elephants. He meant we the people."

"Okay."

"You don't think this is the Lunatic Asylum of the Universe?"

"Kurt, I don't think I expressed an opinion one way or the other."

"We are killing this planet as a life-support system with the poisons from all the thermodynamic whoopee we're making with atomic energy and fossil fuels, and everybody knows it, and practically nobody cares. This is how crazy we are. I think the planet's immune system is trying to get rid of us with AIDS and new strains of flu and tuberculosis, and so on. I think the planet should get rid of us. We're really awful animals. I mean, that dumb Barbra Streisand song, 'People who need people are the luckiest people in the world'—she's talking about cannibals. Lots to eat. Yes, the planet is trying to get rid of us, but I think it's too late."

And I said good-bye to my friend, hung up the phone, sat down and wrote this epitaph: "The good Earth—we could have saved it, but we were too damn cheap and lazy."

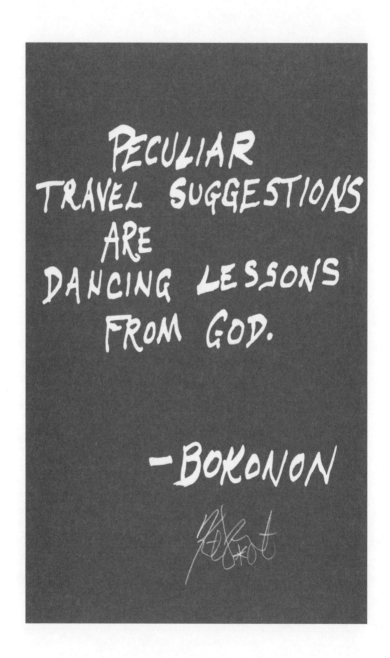

12

I used to be the owner and manager of an automobile dealership in West Barnstable, Massachusetts, called Saab Cape Cod. It and I went out of business thirty-three years ago. The Saab then, as now, was a Swedish car, and I now believe my failure as a dealer so long ago explains what would otherwise remain a deep mystery: Why the Swedes have never given me a Nobel Prize for Literature. Old Norwegian proverb:

"Swedes have short dicks but long memories."

Listen: The Saab back then had only one model, a bug like a VW, a two-door sedan, but with the engine in front. It had suicide doors opening into the slipstream. Unlike all other cars, but like your lawnmower and your outboard, it had a two-stroke rather than a four-stroke engine. So every time you filled your tank with gas, you had to pour in a can of oil as well. For whatever reason, straight women did not want to do this.

The chief selling point was that a Saab could drag a VW at a stoplight. But if you or your significant other had failed to add oil to the last tank of gas, you and the car would then become fireworks. It also had front-wheel drive, of some help on slippery pavements or when accelerating into curves. There was this as well: As one prospective customer said to me, "They make the best watches. Why wouldn't they make the best cars, too?" I was bound to agree.

The Saab back then was a far cry from the sleek, powerful, four-stroke yuppie uniform it is today. It was the wet dream, if you like, of engineers in an airplane factory who'd never made a car before. Wet dream, did I say? Get a load of this: There was a ring on the dashboard, connected to a chain running over pulleys in the engine compartment. Pull on it, and at the far end it would raise a sort of window shade on a spring-loaded roller behind the front grill. That was to keep the engine warm while you went off somewhere. So, when you came back, if you hadn't stayed away too long, the engine would start right up again.

But if you stayed away too long, window shade or not, the oil would separate from the gas and sink like molasses to the bottom of the tank. So when you started up again, you would lay down a smokescreen like a destroyer in a naval engagement. And I actually blacked out the whole town of Woods Hole at high noon that way, having left a Saab in a parking lot there for about a week. I am told old timers there still wonder out loud about where all that smoke could have come from.

I came to speak ill of Swedish engineering, and so diddled myself out of a Nobel Prize.

It's damn hard to make jokes work. In *Cat's Cradle*, for instance, there are these very short chapters. Each one of them represents one day's work, and each one is a joke. If I were writing about a tragic situation, it wouldn't be necessary to time it to make sure the thing works. You can't really misfire with a tragic scene. It's bound to be moving if all the right elements are present. But a joke is like building a mousetrap from scratch. You have to work pretty hard to make the thing snap when it is supposed to snap.

I still listen to comedy, and there's not much of that sort around. The closest thing is the reruns of Groucho Marx's quiz show, *You Bet Your Life*. I've known funny writers who stopped being funny, who became serious persons and could no longer make jokes. I'm thinking of Michael Frayn, the British author who wrote *The Tin Men*. He became a very serious person. Something happened in his head.

Humor is a way of holding off how awful life can be, to protect yourself. Finally, you get just too tired, and the news is too awful, and humor doesn't work anymore. Somebody like Mark Twain thought life was quite awful but held the awfulness at bay with jokes and so forth, but finally he couldn't do it anymore. His wife, his best friend, and two of his daughters had died. If you live long enough, a lot of people close to you are going to die.

It may be that I am no longer able to joke—that it is no longer a satisfactory defense mechanism. Some people are funny, and some are not. I used to be funny, and perhaps I'm not anymore. There may have been so many shocks and disappointments that the defense of humor no longer works. It may be that I have become rather grumpy because I've seen so many things that have offended me that I cannot deal with in terms of laughter.

This may have happened already. I really don't know what I'm going to become from now on. I'm simply along for the ride to see what happens to this body and this brain of mine. I'm startled that I became a writer. I don't think I can control my life or my writing. Every other writer I know feels he is steering himself, and I don't have that feeling. I don't have that sort of control. I'm simply becoming.

All I really wanted to do was give people the relief of laughing. Humor can be a relief, like an aspirin tablet. If a hundred years from now people are still laughing, I'd certainly be pleased.

*

I apologize to all of you who are the same age as my grandchildren. And many of you reading this are probably the same age as my grandchildren.

They, like you, are being royally shafted and lied to by our Baby Boomer corporations and government.

Yes, this planet is in a terrible mess. But it has always been a mess. There have never been any "Good Old Days," there have just been days. And as I say to my grandchildren, "Don't look at me. I just got here."

There are old poops who will say that you do not become a grown-up until you have somehow survived, as they have, some famous calamity— the Great Depression, the Second World War, Vietnam, whatever. Storytellers are responsible for this destructive, not to say suicidal, myth. Again and again in stories, after some terrible mess, the character is able to say at last, "Today I am a woman. Today I am a man. The end."

When I got home from the Second World War, my Uncle Dan clapped me on the back, and he said, "You're a man now." So I killed him. Not really, but I certainly felt like doing it.

Dan, that was my bad uncle, who said a male can't be a man unless he'd gone to war.

But I had a good uncle, my late Uncle Alex. He was my father's kid brother, a childless graduate of Harvard who was an honest life-insurance salesman in Indianapolis. He was well-read and wise. And his principal complaint about other human beings was that they so seldom noticed it when they were happy. So when we were drinking lemonade under an apple tree in the summer, say, and talking lazily about this and that, almost buzzing like honeybees, Uncle Alex would suddenly interrupt the agreeable blather to exclaim, "If this isn't nice, I don't know what is."

So I do the same now, and so do my kids and grandkids. And I urge you to please notice when you are happy, and exclaim or murmur or think at some point, "If this isn't nice, I don't know what is."

We are not born with imagination. It has to be developed by teachers, by parents. There was a time when imagination was very important because it was the major source of entertainment. In 1892 if you were a seven-year-old, you'd read a story—just a very simple one—about a girl whose dog had died. Doesn't that make you want to cry? Don't you know how that little girl feels? And you'd read another story about a rich man slipping on a banana peel. Doesn't that make you want to laugh? And this imagination circuit is being built in your head. If you go to an art gallery, here's just a square with daubs of paint on it that haven't moved in hundreds of years. No sound comes out of it.

The imagination circuit is taught to respond to the most minimal of cues. A book is an arrangement of twenty-six phonetic symbols, ten numerals, and about eight punctuation marks, and people can cast their eyes over these and envision the eruption of Mount Vesuvius or the Battle of Waterloo. But it's no longer necessary for teachers and parents to build these circuits. Now there are professionally produced shows with great actors, very convincing sets, sound, music. Now there's the information highway. We don't need the circuits any more than we need to know how to ride horses. Those of us who had imagination circuits built can look in someone's face and see stories there; to everyone else, a face will just be a face.

And there, I've just used a semi-colon, which at the outset I told you never to use. It is to make a point that I did it. The point is: Rules only take us so far, even good rules.

Who was the wisest person I ever met in my entire life? It was a man, but of course it needn't have been. It was the graphic artist Saul Steinberg, who like everybody else I know, is dead now. I could ask him anything, and six seconds would pass, and then he would give me a perfect answer, gruffly, almost a growl. He was born in Romania, in a house where, according to him, "the geese looked in the windows."

I said, "Saul, how should I feel about Picasso?"

Six seconds passed, and then he said, "God put him on Earth to show us what it's like to be *really* rich."

I said, "Saul, I am a novelist, and many of my friends are novelists and good ones, but when we talk I keep feeling we are in two very different businesses. What makes me feel that way?"

Six seconds passed, and then he said, "It's very simple. There are two sorts of artists, one not being in the least superior to the other. But one responds to the history of his or her art so far, and the other responds to life itself."

I said, "Saul, are you *gifted*?"

Six seconds passed, and then he growled, "No, but what you respond to in any work of art is the artist's struggle against his or her limitations."

82 AS OF
11/11/04

REQUIEM

The crucified planet Earth,
should it find a voice
and a sense of irony,
might now well say
of our abuse of it,
"Forgive them, Father,
They know not what they do."

The irony would be
that we know what
we are doing.

When the last living thing
has died on account of us,
how poetical it would be
if Earth could say,
in a voice floating up
perhaps
from the floor
of the Grand Canyon,
"It is done."
People did not like it here.

AUTHOR'S NOTE

The full-page, hand-lettered statements scattered throughout this book, "samplers suitable for framing" if you like, are pictures of products of Origami Express, a business partnership between myself and Joe Petro III, with headquarters in Joe's painting and silk-screening studio in Lexington, Kentucky. I paint or draw pictures, and Joe makes prints of some of them, one by one, color by color, by means of the time-consuming, archaic silk screen process, practiced by almost nobody else any more: squeegeeing inks through cloths and onto paper. This process is so painstaking and tactile, almost balletic, that each print Joe makes is a painting in its own right.

Our partnership's name, Origami Express, is my tribute to the many-layered packages Joe makes for prints he sends for me to sign and number. The logo for Origami, made by Joe, isn't his picture of a picture I sent him, but of a picture by me that he found in my novel *Breakfast of Champions*. It is of a bomb in air, on its way down, with these words written on its side:

GOODBYE

BLUE

MONDAY

I have to have been one of the luckiest persons alive, since I have survived for four score and two years now. I can't begin to count all the times I should have been dead or wished I were. But one of the best things that ever happened to me, a one-in-a-billion opportunity to enjoy myself in perfect innocence, was my meeting Joe.

Here's the thing: Back in 1993, almost eleven years ago now, I was scheduled to lecture on November 1 at Midway College, a women's school on the edge of Lexington. Well in advance of my appearance, a Kentucky artist, Joe Petro III, son of the Kentucky artist Joe Petro II, asked me to do a black-and-white self-portrait, which he could then use in silk-screen posters to be used by the school. So I did and he did. Joe was only thirty-seven back then, and I was a mere spring chicken of only seventy-one, not even twice his age.

When I got down there to speak, and was so happy about the posters, I learned from Joe himself that he painted romantic but scientifically precise pictures of wildlife, from which he made silk screen images. He had majored in zoology at the University of Tennessee. Yes, and some of his pictures were so appealing and informative that they had been used as propaganda by Greenpeace, an organization trying, with scant success so far, to prevent the murder of species, even our own, by the way we live now. And Joe, having shown me the poster and his own work and his studio, said to me in effect, "Why don't we keep on going?"

And so we have, and it seems quite possible in retrospect that Joe Petro III saved my life. I will not explain. I will let it go at that.

We have since collaborated on more than two hundred different images, with Joe making editions, signed and numbered by me, of ten or more of each of them. The "samplers" in this book are not at all representative of our total oeuvre, but are simply very recent *jeux d'esprit*. Most of our stuff has been my knockoffs of Paul Klee and Marcel Duchamp and so on.

And since we first met, Joe has beguiled others into sending him pictures for him to do with what he so much loves to do. Among them are the comedian Jonathan Winters, an art student long ago, and the English artist Ralph Steadman, whose accomplishments include the appropriately harrowing illustrations for Hunter Thompson's *Fear and Loathing* books. And Steadman and I have come to know and like each other on account of Joe.

Yes, and last July (2004) there was an exhibition of Joe's and my stuff, arranged by Joe, at the Indianapolis Art Center in the town of my birth. But there was also a painting by my architect and painter grandfather Bernard Vonnegut, and two by my architect and painter father Kurt Vonnegut, and six apiece by my daughter Edith and my son the doctor Mark.

Ralph Steadman heard about this family show

from Joe and sent me a note of congratulation. I wrote him back as follows: "Joe Petro III staged a reunion of four generations of my family in Indianapolis, and he has made you and me feel like first cousins. Is it possible that he is God? We could do worse."

Only kidding, of course.

Are Origami's pictures any good? Well, I asked the now regrettably dead painter Syd Solomon, a most agreeable neighbor on Long Island for many summertimes, how to tell a good picture from a bad one. He gave me the most satisfactory answer I ever expect to hear. He said, "Look at a million pictures, and you can never be mistaken."

I passed this on to my daughter Edith, a professional painter, and she too thought it was pretty good. She said she "could rollerskate through the Louvre, saying, 'Yes, no, no, yes, no, yes,' and so on."

Okay?

KURT VONNEGUT is among the few grandmasters of American letters, one without whom the very term American literature would mean much less than it does. He was born in Indianapolis, Indiana, on November 11, 1922. Vonnegut lives in New York City and Bridgehampton, New York, with his wife, the author and photographer Jill Krementz.

To see more of Kurt Vonnegut's original art, visit www.vonnegut.com.